AND SHORT
THE SEASON

ALSO BY MAXINE KUMIN

AND SHORT
THE SEASON

poems

Maxine Kumin

W. W. NORTON & COMPANY

NEW YORK • LONDON

For information about permission to reproduce selections from this book,
write to Permissions, W. W. Norton & Company, Inc.,
500 Fifth Avenue, New York, NY 10110

For information about special discounts for bulk purchases,
please contact W. W. Norton Special Sales at
specialsales@wwnorton.com or 800-233-4830

Manufacturing by Courier Westford
Book design by Devon Zahn and Rebecca Caine
Production manager: Devon Zahn

Library of Congress Cataloging-in-Publication Data

Kumin, Maxine, date.
[Poems. Selections]
And short the season : poems / Maxine Kumin. — First Edition.
pages cm
ISBN 978-0-393-24100-6 (hardcover)
I. Title.
PS3521.U638A6 2014
811'.54—dc23

2013041178

W. W. Norton & Company, Inc.
500 Fifth Avenue, New York, N.Y. 10110
www.wwnorton.com

W. W. Norton & Company Ltd.
Castle House, 75/76 Wells Street, London W1T 3QT

2 3 4 5 6 7 8 9 0

for JUDITH

CONTENTS

ACKNOWLEDGMENTS

Grateful thanks to the editors where these poems first appeared or were anthologized. Warm thanks also to Elizabeth Marshall Thomas for permission to lineate a prose selection from *The Old Way* as "The Women Return from Digging Roots in the Kalahari," and for the last line of "Wellfleet, Cape Cod," from the same source.

The Atlantic
The Bark
bosque
The Georgia Review
Green Mountains Review
Hudson Review
New Letters
The New Yorker
The New York Times
Paterson Literary Review
Ploughshares
Poet Lore
Poetry
Prairie Schooner
River Styx
Southern Poetry Review

"Either Or" was published in *The Best American Poetry 2012*, edited by Mark Doty (Scribner, 2012).

"William Carlos Williams" was published in *Visiting Dr. Williams: Poems Inspired by the Life and Work of William Carlos Williams*, edited by Thom Tammaro (University of Iowa Press, 2011).

"Just Deserts" was published in *Saying What Happened: American Poetry after the Millennium*, edited by Ann Keniston and Jeffrey Gray (McFarland & Co., Jefferson N.C., 2012).

"The Last Good War" was published in *Sisters: An Anthology*, edited by Jan Freeman, Emily Wojcik, and Deborah Bull (Paris Press, 2010).

"Sonnets Uncorseted" appeared in *Shakespeare's Sisters: Voices of English and European Women* (Folger Shakespeare Library, Washington, D.C., 2012).

"The Revisionist Dream," inadvertently omitted from *Where I Live: Selected Poems 1990–2010*, is reprinted here from *Still to Mow*, 2007.

AND SHORT
THE SEASON

I

WHEREOF THE GIFT IS SMALL

Henry Howard, Earl of Surrey

And short the season, first rubythroat
in the fading lilacs, alyssum in bloom,
a honeybee bumbling in the bleeding heart
on my gelding's grave while beetles swarm
him underground. Wet feet, wet cuffs,
little flecks of buttercup on my sneaker toes,
bluets, violets crowding out the tufts
of rich new grass the horses nose
and nibble like sleepwalkers held fast—
brittle beauty—might this be the last?

THE PATH, THE CHAIR

Walking the fields before the first snow
silently saying my breviary of poems:
Yeats's *Easter*, Auden's *September*,
reams of Wordsworth's *Intimations*
who walked more miles than Lamb or Hazlitt,
even outwalked indefatigable Coleridge,
I side with these Romantic democrats,
a point of pride to wind their way shanks mare
through the Wenlock and Quantock Hills.
Like Housman, Will composed in his head
humming his lines as long as his feet
could hold the rhythm on the path.

Forty years of trudging the bounds
of our fields. Alps One and Two we fenced
by hand, posthole digger, cedar posts,
three-board fencing seeking out
the level of the slope. These give way
to what the British call a steep.
Darkly shaded, gravelly, the ominous
overflow of a brook has earned it
the sobriquet The Dragon Pit for the way

the horses stopped in daily terror, then
galloped through up into the sunlit sprawl
of Field Three, once fenced in wire,
now strictly held by Nature.

Three overlooks The Pear Tree Field,
where a single wild Bartlett stands
freed from the smother of brambles,
beyond the stone wall that once served
to keep sheep fast. Climbing again,
our outermost and final summer pasture,
The Elysian Field, dotted with granite
outcrops that invite the passerby
to pause, climb up, take in the view,
the humps and bumps of distant hills,
admire the stream bisecting it,
the homemade run-in shed that holds the winter sun.

A woodland path from there, soft underfoot
with forest duff, corkscrews among
benign and moribund red pine pillars
planted by the CCC in the Depression

but never harvested. Ahead lies table land
300 feet above the house
and nothing fancy, raised beds cobbled
from hemlock boards now bulging
from the press of ancient manure where corn
and beans, leeks, beets and carrots prosper.
The fence around, lopsided chicken wire
buried as deep as we could force it,
topped with split boards silvered gray,
the gate proud to be made from salvaged scraps
and always the chitter of returning birds,
mostly yellow warblers though each year
their numbers diminish, along with their habitat.

My resting place, from which I watch
the rhubarb swell, the peas inch up,
the early spinach break through clods,
a folding chair once formed of crisscrossed plastic,
all dissolved except the metal frame until we wove
both seat and back from baling twine saved from
the squares of hay that fed the growing herd.
Saving is a form of worship: the restored fields,
the rescued dogs, the ancient horses

named Genesis and Deuteronomy,
Eden, Praise Be, Hallelujah, and the farthest field
saluting the Greek gods and goddesses,
our catholic homage to an afterlife
we like the thought of but don't believe in.

A DAY'S WORK

remembering Barbara Swan

Those great flat stumps in the forest
ringed with a dozen saplings desperate
to become trees in their own right

at first seem blessed with bright intelligence
then bend aimlessly in the wind
drop their buds and are reabsorbed.

Long ago the raw wood of a day's work
was lugged out by draft horse or ox
and their dung moldered in the forest duff

feeding the ancient mycorrhizal paths
where clusters of honey mushrooms scattered
the talc of their spores each September

and do so year after year whether or not
I come to forage among these slabs in the clearing
where men and animals sweated together.

Plucking today's flush, I salute the artist
whose pen-and-ink sketch of *armillaria*
hangs on my study wall, how she reported

she drew three versions of our day's pickings
here fifty-five years ago, then *took them home*
cooked 'em up and et 'em.

OUR MANTLE

A small bit of soil
perfectly formed and
untouched by the plow
once turned over
becomes a bed of clods.

When wetted down
from it arises
delicious briefest
petrichor, the scent
of new rain on dry earth.

This is the *regolith*
the duvet of dust, dirt,
gravel, sand, mud
which may have been
just deposited

or may go back
hundreds of millions of years
as it does in the Australian
outback, taken for
granted, self-evident cover

like skin over flesh
and sin under always
pumping out oil
pumping in poison
fracking our planet

our *mantle*
resting on bedrock.

PURIM AND THE BEETLES
OF OUR LADY

My love for this earth goes beyond thought,
a fan writes me and so does mine, except for
coleomegilla maculata, these beetles of Our Lady
that saved Mary's garden from mealybugs in
medieval times. They emerge in a moment of melt
to slip into our homes through crevices too slight
for a whisper, *coleomegilla,* surely not

from the rescued yiddish of my father—
megillah for a lengthy convoluted story,
retold at the feast of Purim, suspense
and revenge in the telling: Queen Esther,
Uncle Mordecai, and Haman the villain
to be read on the eleventh day of Adar,
not too early in the calendar for these

ten-spotted bloodlets dropping into dinner,
swarming the globe light over the table,
crowding the mullions in morning sunlight,
our commonest ladybug, which Spellcheck
will redo as *communist,* not a bad word choice
for these hordes to be vacuumed up and expelled
naked in the snow or in the compost barrel, but

do I love this earth enough to store them
in ladybug houses available online, free shipping,
until the spring month of Adar is over, then
unleash them to feast in my vegetable garden
on the species that riddle the leafy crops?
Let us reflect on Haman the evil one
the Agagite in Persia under King Xerxes

in the fifth century B.C., now called
before the common era, which is not before
ladybugs first hatched. Consider the orphan
Queen Esther who has married Ahasuerus
the king, consider the good uncle Mordecai
who urges her to foil the plot against her people
by revealing her origins—until then unknown.
Oh what a megillah long before the story
of Mary rescued from mealybugs by
coleomegilla maculata, long before beetles
began to eat holes in my love for this earth.

DISCRETE ACTIVITIES

The cloacal kiss between turkeys
seemingly awkward, still
makes more turkeys.
Every morning

a trail of poults in tow,
the wild flock courses
across the manure pile
to peck the redelivered seeds

and because she would
not stand to be bred
the mare received
the stallion's semen,

ejaculated in a false
vagina, via turkey baster
to make the foal she
nuzzles and gives suck

while the bird-dung spider
weaves an imitation
dropping on a leaf,
then lays her egg

dead center: discrete
activities, yet all
connected by what
the poet wrote:

*life will do anything
for a living.*

INDIAN PIPES

The vision of her thrashing
scrabbling for footing then

    falling back—two hours of this until
    the vet's pentobarbital releases her—

how prettily we decorate the grave, ring
it with smooth stones, plant lilies when

    what it wants, this rotting body lying
    under our fossicking, is the corpse plant

each stem putting up its solitary
nodding dead white flower, sometimes

    displaying a pinkish Caucasian flesh tone,
    evolved during the Jurassic, trampled

by dinosaurs, older and ghostlier than
fox-size deer-fleet eohippus fusing his hind three,

    front four fingers into hooves long after
    the death of dinosaurs, rising in the Eocene

when the white wraiths grew among bitter russulas
and lactarias, mycorrhizal with numinous trees

in mossy groves, oh old two-thousand-mile
contrary overloved game mare, I would

dig deep through centuries of forest duff
to lay you here. Begin again.

THE FURTIVE VISIT

We opened the foxed pages of our hearts
back, further back, and let them stand,
climbed through mild rain to the nippled pond,
clung in a wet embrace, then drew apart.

I watched the tailights judder as you took
the downhill elbows of the mudslicked lane
minutes shy of midnight. Not again,
I thought, whistling the dogs back in,

the rain now picking up its steady redirect.

ELEGY BEGINNING WITH HALF A LINE
FROM BEN JONSON

Dry, bald, and sere
my old college roommate dead of cancer
keeps walking into my midnights where

we're heading north again from White River
two girls thumbing by the highway never
molested not even propositioned by delivery-

men who stop to ask us where the hell we're going
—to her parents' place—and next we're galloping
her mother's horses one hot yellow afternoon

until their flanks lather and their nostrils flare
we swim them right into the cobblestoned river
nevermind soaking the expensive British leather

cool now drinking spiked punch at the college Jolly-Ups
we're proud of getting seasoned making out among the wraps
on someone's Ash Street bed the sun's eclipse

through smoked glass smoking Parliaments and pot
we are forming our selves—what tamed us? not
the KGB the CIA the FBI but time that cat

burglar it's dawn I curse your cunning stalker cancer
four five six chemos carry off your zest your hair
radiation strips your frame nevermind you swear

even morphined that you'll beat him all hollow
and then you swim your sweaty horse up to Valhalla.

ROSIE SPEAKS

shriven: to have obtained absolution

Now that I'm gone perhaps they'll forgive my sins—
those times I woke in the night and trotted
downstairs to relieve myself—not only of urine—
on the guest room rug; they'll allow me the junco I caught

and swallowed whole except for a last indigest-
ible feather; grant me the chipmunk that followed,
its tail protruding, until with a final gust
I managed to get it down, harshly swallowed.

Aren't these mere peccadilloes compared to my gifts?
When green beans were topped and tailed wasn't
I there to search and destroy the stray bits?
I was the secret snorkeler, the pointy-nosed peasant

who served under the table at meals, who leapt
into laps at leisure, or performed when the cue was given,
rolling over and over, delighting the guests.
Wasn't I ever the darling? Tell me I'm shriven.

THE LUXURY

Right now
at four below zero I have the luxury
of not knowing if the six dogs chained
to their ramshackle doghouses are lying
on hay from the old bale I took to their owner
this morning with the admonition that all dogs
confined out of doors deserve to have
dry bedding.

I have the luxury
of not knowing when they were last fed
or of not seeing where the five children
sleep or what covers them or how their father
serving a year in the House of Correction
for petty larceny and public drunkenness
is being corrected. All of us neighbors
who have fought with the town for years
to take action have the luxury.

We have
called the police, the selectmen, the state vet,
the SPCA, the Department of Public Health
the Division of Child and Youth Protection Services.
The judge, well known to us as a feckless
and pleasant servant of the law soon to retire
on a fixed guaranteed income, keeps
taking this ancient case under advisement.
He too has the luxury of unknowing.

II

ANCIENT HISTORY
IN THE EYE CENTER

Loud enough for Stentor himself, the waiting-room
video recycles hour after hour the same
weary sequence reciting the grim

signs of glaucoma, advising Restasis
to increase tear production, praising
the League of the Legally Blind, which is

what I am in one eye, the bad eye, as if it had done
something wrong and needed to be punished every month.
Somewhere I read that in an ancient kingdom

victors gouged out the eyes of nine
captives in each group of ten, leaving one
sighted soldier to pick the way home,

a vision that stays with me as antibiotic drops
alternate with numbing ones. Then come swabs
of Betadine and with one stroke my chair collapses

to lay me flat, the medieval metal pry
applied to hold this bad eye
open and I begin to hy-

perventilate knowing the needle is next,
hearing the retinologist flick
the barrel of the hypodermic

to expel the fleck of air bubble
before he plunges it into my eyeball.
More Q-tip swabbings. Last of all

donning his miner's lamp he leans over me
asking can I see a bright light? Can I see
it? Can I ever find the way

home? Does he fear he has rendered me blind?
In the war against Spartacus decimation
bludgeoned to death one out of every ten men.

Crucified thousands lined the Appian
Way in 91 B.C. from Rome to Capua,
phantasms that assault me, left supine

to marinate for half an hour.
A techie comes to check my ocular
pressure. Released, I breathe out *au revoir.*

MURDER

At Sunday supper my father
already in pajamas and slippers
after his deep-sea bath in
the oldfashioned tub on clawfeet
said ruefully—at least I thought
it was rueful—
Well, I murdered this day.

Beached in bed until 7,
he broke his fast with lamb chops
and lolled all morning in his Barcalounger
consuming *The New York Times.*
In the afternoon in clement weather
he sauntered around his bailiwick.

Six days a week he rose at dawn.
He drove from his shiny white suburb
to South Philadelphia where
he took his rightful place behind
the counter of his pawnshop. At night
he soaked his sore feet
in a fragrant broth of witch hazel.

I want to tell him that I too
murdered this day, I slumped at my desk
over unborn poems adding
a word here, half a line there
but mostly deleting, deleting, deleting
in an ecstasy of failure.

At midday, clement or not
I walked with the dogs up the woods road
to the garden and pond.
Sometimes a great blue heron
flapped up from his illicit fishing.
Sometimes it rained or snowed.

Back at the desk I worried
another essay the world does not need
on aspects of the variable foot
in the poetry of William
Carlos Williams.
Before bed I iced my sore foot.

Fellow murderer,
lie back in your worn plush chair.
Ignore the halogen filament
that shines on my scratch and scribble.
Let us be rueful together.

RADFORD, VIRGINIA, 1904

The god of chance plucked this kodak print
from a caved-in box of lost ancestors
born in the blear of the Hapsburg twilight.

My mother's three youngest brothers balance
astride her father's prize Saddlebred

the mount most favored by Civil War generals:
Grant, Stonewall Jackson, and Lee.

The muscular stableboy, shirtsleeves rolled
cap cocked back on his head
two generations up from slavery

hooks a casual finger under the halter
to show that this horse does not need to be held.

Grandfather, now the proprietor
of the fusty drygoods store on the square

drives his highstepping bay down the narrow
dirt roads out of Radford, but only on Sunday
afternoons, so as not to offend the churchy.

There goes the jew, they say of his clatter
nothing remarking the forty-day crossing

his father made, fifty years ago
to escape being pressed into Metternich's army

or his plod heading south out of Baltimore
pack on his back, an itinerant peddler.
Forgotten, the uniforms that he stitched

for the Confederates, the nest egg he lost.
Nothing deploring the gradual fade

of the smooth-gaited Saddlebreds
long preferred on Southern plantations
now being displaced by the horseless carriage

making its shaky uncertain way
on a new road surface called macadam.

Three little boys on a statuesque horse
while Radford is linked by the telephone
—Bell calls it "the harmonic telegraph"—

to Lynchburg and Blacksburg and Roanoke
and soon enough the world.

THE REVISIONIST DREAM

Well, she didn't kill herself that afternoon.
It was a mild day in October, we sat outside
over sandwiches. She said she had begun

to practice yoga, take piano lessons,
rewrite her drama rife with lust and pride
and so she didn't kill herself that afternoon,

hugged me, went home, cranked the garage doors open,
scuffed through the garish leaves, orange and red,
that brought on grief. She said she had begun

to translate Akhmatova, her handsome Russian
piano teacher rendering the word-for-word
so she didn't kill herself that afternoon.

She cooked for him, made quiche and coq au vin.
He stood the Czerny method on its head
while her fingers flew. She said she had begun

accelerandos, Julia Child, and some
expand-a-lung deep breaths to do in bed
so she didn't kill herself that afternoon.
We ate our sandwiches. The dream blew up at dawn.

TAKEN INSIDE

This is the beauty of books. They arrive
inside us in the most peculiar ways
wrote Colum McCann who so loved
James Joyce that he ate a flake
of the first edition of *Ulysses*
that had fallen onto the blue cloth
in a private nook of the Berg Collection
Reading Room where he could look
but not touch.

I learned to read and write. I learned
who made the world? God. Also
how to pray the rosary. To this day
I can say it straight through, bead by bead
the only Jewish child at the Convent
of the Sisters of St. Joseph next door.
At the end of the corridor a twice-
lifesize Jesus to my horror
hung in pain.

This was before the long yellow buses.
My parents discussed public school
a mile away, too far for the youngest
child and only girl to walk alone.
One day longing put my bad
right hand in my classmate's desk.
That night in bed rolling the beads
I told the rosary and fell asleep
blessed by Jesus.

But where was He the next day when
thief was a word nailed to me? I walked
the lonely mile uphill to third grade.
Tragic queen, I was ahead in all
subjects. I could write cursive,
do long division, knew the words
to two verses of our national anthem,
Jesus no longer my
special friend.

THE BIRD, THE COURT OF
COMMON PLEAS, THE CZAR

The prothonotary warbler, small
chrome yellow singer of the hardwood swamps,
named by the bayou Creoles after
the golden robes of the *protonotarii*,
chief advisors to the Pope,
caught my child-eye with its lemony brilliance
long before I could puzzle out its name.

How odd to find this esoteric word again
on my father's father's citizenship diploma
when in 1888, still more boy than man,
he rose before the office of the Prothonotary
of the Court of Common Pleas in Philadelphia
—said to be the oldest legal seat
in the western hemisphere—to declare

that it was bona fide his intent
to renounce forever all allegiance
to any foreign prince or potentate
or sovereignty of whatsoever state
and particularly to the Czar
of Russia, the Czar, the hated murderer,
the first of whom is shown mitered

and sceptered, scarved in orange yellow
following his coronation in 913.
The last, deprived of butter, croissants and coffee,
is shot in a basement room with his wife, son,
four daughters, doctor, footman and chef
in 1918, shorn of his golden epaulettes.
He, Nicholas II, Prothonotary of pogroms.

THE LAST GOOD WAR

Pearl Harbor. A scurry to marry. Two brothers
take up with a pair of sweet Southern sisters.
Antebellum manners, mouths that plaster rumors
on the brothers' sister, younger than summer.
They never aspired to the Seven Sisters.
Claim she is sleeping with her professor.

When the pater familias bursts a main artery
leaving a tangled will, read the next chapter
in the lives of two brothers who married two sisters.
Imagine which sister unties the tether,
which couple keeps the house with wisteria
twining the back fence they bought together.

Brothers, oh brothers, how could you go bitter,
go without speaking, one winner, one debtor?
Less than a year fells taker and giver
but the widows remain, their old quarrels fester
as into their nineties they flourish, the sisters
whose sweet Southern manners won them two brothers.

THE STANDING ROAST

Long after swearing off
eating red meat, juices
still flood my mouth
remembering how it came
to the table wreathed about
with parsley and carrots
and each of us four kids
hoseying a rib to gnaw on.

Old orphan, I unearth
my father's bonehandled knife
the blade become a scimitar
from years of whetting and
as I raise it blood
leaks from the first cut.

WELLFLEET, CAPE COD

*Lionesses do almost all of the hunting. They creep stealthily
through vegetation and leap upon their unsuspecting prey.*
Defenders of Wildlife

That frantic time we found the children
in a sweet-smelling heap in the dune grass
sprawled and vulnerable, the oldest one dozy,
the younger two deeply asleep after
an idyllic July afternoon, how tenderly
you untangled them, lifting the boy
to your shoulders, cupping the girl
in your arms as I whispered the eldest awake
and we formed a silent procession
back to the little cottage.

Of course the lioness would have eaten the children
if she found them huddled asleep on the veldt
all but invisible in the tall grasses while
we searched for them calling and calling . . .

Instead, all five settled at sundown, I poured
the wine, you pried open the oysters
we had wrenched from the rocks at low tide
not knowing the children had gone missing.

At midnight I saw the lioness. Her eyes were
two little green moons shining in the darkness.

NO PLACE

*We have found the nearest thing
to paradise on earth,* wrote Elisabeth,
Friedrich Nietzsche's sister, who
fled her fatherland in 1887 for
Nueva Germania, a colony
in Paraguay of racially

pure anti-Semitic vegetarians
or were they purely Aryan
vegetarian anti-Semites?
Her husband, the founder, two
years later killed himself
the hard way, taking poison.

Everything they planted failed
except manioc which was only good
for tapioca and ideology died away
as Guarani Indians and Latins
cohabitated with a dozen of the bigots
on the hot plains of San Pedro.

Auschwitz's Angel of Death Mengele
came by much later hiding out
after gassing all my father's kin.
Is this what happens to utopias
from the Greek *outopos*, no place,
why must they all evolve from *u*- to *dys*-?

Even in my Jewish atheistic all-organic
vegetable garden where wild dill
used to outwit the squash bugs
and beneficial insects guarded the beans
this year the corn succumbed to earworm.
Hard rains hatched battalions of slugs.

The onions rotted, the carrots were raddled
with root maggots, the purple pole beans collapsed.
Fieldmice had a field day, raccoons a coon fest.
The deer came in, it was a paradise
for beasts, another earthly day for us.
No Paraguayan bliss, no Nazis on the lam.

NATIONAL VELVET

When the Vatican charged Elizabeth Taylor
with erotic vagrancy in 1962 for sleeping
with Richard Burton while still married to
I forget who, there were so many, all
I could think of was her soaring over fences
on The Pie, her first love, a piebald horse
with one blue eye who'd leapt a five-foot
stone wall to get into another pasture
and one thing led to another in the book
by Enid Bagnold and Liz rose to stardom
in Hollywood at age twelve. Piebalds
have large patches, usually black on white,
sometimes the other way around, which are not
desirable on a thoroughbred, especially
one with eyes that do not match, two
traits suggesting some erotic vagrancy—
a hybrid rogue slipped generations back
into the registry. Liz married seven men,
Burton twice, by which time he was losing
his hair and she was growing a double chin,
but let us remember how fiercely she flew
over fences on the wild piebald horse
with one brown eye and one that was blue.

III

OLD NEWS

Medic Recalls Detainee Chained to Cage
Like laundry, draped in neat pentameter.

He tended bullet wounds in the teenager's
Back twice daily in a five-foot square

Crate at a U.S. lockup at Bagram.
The Pentagon defended what was done

To the chained and hooded prisoner
As sactioned punishment of young Khadr.

The medic didn't object; chaining was approved.
He borrowed him to translate for other captives.

He didn't inquire how long they let him hang.
Shackled, the boy soiled himself. Beatings.

Threats of rape. Solitary. Prolonged cold.
It only makes page 6. The news is old.

The New York Times,
May 4, 2010; July 11, 2008

RED TAPE AND KANGAROO COURTS I

On this tropical refrigerated paved-over island
where banana rats are rampant

endangered species iguanas dine on
McDonald's and Subway discards

and the list of things that are prohibited
in the camps is itself prohibited

—not Kafka but George Clarke, a tax lawyer
working pro bono at Guantánamo

where special clearance and special papers
required to reach this "theater" are months in coming

where Arabic-speaking inmates are pressed to serve
with no skilled translators available

and capital cases are heard with no
capital defense attorneys allowed

RED TAPE AND KANGAROO COURTS II

Soundproof glass between
the accused and observers in the courtroom

shields what cannot be said
what must be interrupted if the detainees

speak of the dark acts at the dark
heart of what took place during their confinement:

for interrogation they held his head in
the toilet and flushed it over and over

for hunger strike they forcefed him until he vomited, then
fed him again until he vomited again

and when he passed out, they doused him awake in a cell
with a steel bunk, no mattress, no blanket

if we don't talk about the torture
it never happened.

The titles and key phrases embedded in these two
sonnets are excerpted from *The Guantánamo Lawyers*,
edited by Mark P. Denbeaux and Jonathan Hafetz
(New York University Press, 2009).

THE PRE-TRIAL CONFINEMENT
OF PRIVATE BRADLEY MANNING

To drive a man to suicide you put
Him on suicide watch, you take away
His sheet and pillow, all his clothes except
His underwear, you shine a light in day

And night, you confiscate his eyeglasses,
Then you deny that he's in solitary.
You say *he lives in his own cell.* Sightless.
Each day he gets to walk around an empty

Room for an hour. No pushups, no jogging in place.
He's not the first one held as an example.
Amnesty reports it seeks redress
As month by month both mind and body crumple.

The Marines treat every detainee
Firmly, fairly, and with dignity.

The New York Times, January 26, 2011

SONNETS UNCORSETED

1.

She was twenty-two. He was fifty-three,
a duke, a widower with ten children.

They met in Paris, each in exile from
the English Civil War. Virginal

and terrified, still she agreed
to marry him. Though women were mere chattel

spinsterhood made you invisible
in the sixteen hundreds. Marriage was arranged

—hers a rare exception. Despite a dowry
a woman never could own property.

Your womb was just for rent. Birth control
contrivances—a paste of ants, cow dung

mashed with honey, tree bark with pennyroyal—
all too often failed the applicant.

Margaret Lucas
marries William
Cavendish, Duke
of Newcastle-upon-
Tyne, in Paris, 1645

2.

If anything went wrong you bled to death.
You bore & bore & bore as you were taught
screaming sometimes for days in childbirth.
To bring forth was a woman's fate

but not for Margaret Cavendish, childless
Duchess of Newcastle. After the head
of Charles the First had been detached
and the Restoration seated a new monarch,

she and the Duke returned to his estate
where nothing discomposed their paradise.
How rare, two lovers scribbling away,
admiring each other's words in privacy.
He: polymath, equestrian, playwright.
She: philosopher, fantasist, poet.

3.

His the first book on the art of dressage,
till then an untried humane approach
to teaching classic paces in the manège,
the grace of the levade and the piaffe.

*Méthode et invention
nouvelle de dresser les
chevaux*, 1658

Hers the goofy utopian fantasy,
The Blazing-World. The heroine is adrift
with her kidnapper in a wooden skiff.
A storm comes up conveniently, and they
are blown to the North Pole. He freezes to death
but she is carried to a contiguous
North Pole, a new world where the emperor
falls in love with her, makes her his empress

1666

and cedes her all his powers over
clans of wildly invented creatures.

4.

Poems, plays, philosophical
discourses on *Platonick* love,   1668
a chapter on her *Birth, Breeding, and Life*   1656
and an *Apology for Writing So Much
Upon this Book* about herself,
even some inquiries into science . . .
years in chosen isolation the Duchess
filled with words, and the Duke with reassurance.

Even this outburst did not discomfit him:
Men are so unconscionable and cruel   Oration of Divers
. . . they *would fain Bury us in their* . . . *beds as in*   Sorts, 1662
a grave . . . *[T]he truth is, we live like Bats or Owls,
Labour like Beasts, and die like Worms.* Pepys
called her *mad, conceited, and ridiculous.*

5.

Virginia Woolf, in 1928,
found her *Quixotic and high-spirited*
as well as somewhat *crack-brained and bird-witted*
but went on to see in her *a vein*
of *authentic fire*. Eighty-odd years on,
flamboyant, eccentric, admittedly vain,

*A Room of One's
Own*, 1928

now she's a respected foremother among
women of letters. Founded in 1997,
the Margaret Cavendish Society
—"international, established to provide
communication between scholars worldwide"—
is plumped with learned papers, confabs, dues.
She's an aristocrat who advocates
—words worn across centuries—for women's rights.

In Oxford, UK

6.

I went to college in the nineteen forties
read Gogol, Stendhal, Zola and Flaubert.
Read Pushkin, Tolstoy, Dostoevsky
and wrote exams that asked: contrast and compare.

Male novelists, male profs, male tutors, not
a single woman on the faculty
nor was there leaven found among the poets
I read and loved: G. M. Hopkins, A. E.
Housman, Auden, Yeats, only Emily
(not quite decoded or yet in the canon).
Ten years later, I struggled to break in
the almost all-male enclave of poetry.

Here's a small glimpse into the hierarchy:
famed Robert Lowell praising Marianne

7.

as the best woman poet in America, put down
by Langston Hughes, bless his egalitarian
soul, who rose at the dinner to pronounce
her the best Negro woman poet in the nation.

Poetry Society of
America banquet,
1967

Terrified of writing *domestic* poems,
poems pungent with motherhood, anathema
to the prevailing clique of male pooh-bahs,
somehow I balanced teaching freshman comp
half-time with kids, meals, pets, errands, spouse.
I wrote in secret, read drafts on the phone
with another restless mother, Anne Sexton,
and *poco a poco* our poems filled up the house.

Tufts University,
1957–59

Then one of us sold a poem to *The New Yorker.*
A week later, the other was welcomed into *Harper's.*

8.

But even as we published our first books
the visiting male bards required care.
We drove them to their readings far and near,

Sexton, *To Bedlam and Part Way Back*, 1960

Kumin, *Halfway*, 1961

thence to the airport just in time to make
their flight to the next gig. *You drive like a man,*
they said by way of praise, and if a poem

of ours seemed worthy they said, *you write like a man.*
When asked what woman poet they read, with one
voice they declaimed, Emily Dickinson.

Saintly Emily safely dead, modern
women poets were dismissed as immature,
their poems pink with the glisten of female organs.

The virus of their disdain hung in the air
but women were now infected with ambition.

9.

We didn't merely saunter decade by decade.
We swept on past de Beauvoir and Friedan,
and took courage from Carolyn Kizer's knife-blade
Pro Femina: *I will speak about women*
of letters for I'm in the racket, urging,
Stand up and be hated, and swear not to sleep with editors.

Composed 1953,
published several
years later

If a woman is to write, Virginia Woolf
has Mary Beton declare, she has to have
five hundred a year and a room with a lock on the door,
a sacred space where Shakespeare's sister Judith
might have equaled his prodigious gift
or not. She might have simply floated there,
set loose in the privilege of privacy, her self
unwritten, under no one else's eyes.

In *A Room of
One's Own*, 1928

10.

Oh, Duchess, come hurdle five centuries
to a land of MFA's in poetry,
of journals in print and even more online,
small presses popping up like grapes on vines,
readings taking place in every cranny,
prizes for first books, some with money.

Come to this apex of tenured women professors
where issues of gender and race fill whole semesters
and students immerse themselves in women's studies.
Meet famous poets who are also unabashed mothers
or singletons by choice or same-sex partners—
black, Latina, Asian, Native American,
white, Christian, Muslim, Jew and atheist—
come join us, Duchess Margaret Cavendish.

IV

AT THE END

I always knew in my heart Walt Whitman's mind to be
more like my own than any other man's living. As he is a
very great scoundrel this is not a pleasant confession.

Gerard Manley Hopkins
in a letter to Robert Bridges

Walt came to see him on his deathbed.
Churned across the English countryside
past coal pits and sulphurous factories
and then across rough waters, greasy-
black crests breaking on the gunwales, to
typhoid-ridden Dublin. It can't be you,
Gerard kept saying as the gay
giant knelt beside his cot,
took his hand and raised it to his lips
whispering, I came to kiss a Jesuit.
I am so happy, Gerard half wept,
so happy here, the two of us . . .
and slipped away delirious.

XANTHOPSIA

It wasn't absinthe or digitalis
in the Yellow House the two of them shared
that led him to layer the chrome coronas
or yellow the sheets in the bedroom in Arles
or tinge the towel negligently hung
on the hook by the door, or yellow the window,
be it distant view or curtain, yolk-lick
the paintings on the wall by the monkish bed.
No, it wasn't sunstroke or the bright light
of southern France that yellowed the café terrace
at the Place du Forum, a pigment
intensified by the little white tables, the white stars
in a blue sky, the deep saffron floor, it wasn't
some chemical or physical insult that stained
the vase with twelve sunflowers a urinous
yellow, the water in the vase yellow,
also the table under the vase—such
a troubled life of yellow leading up
to Vincent's hurled wineglass arousing
Gauguin's rapier to sever his best friend's left ear,
the story they made up that Vincent lopped it
off himself, wrapped it, ran down the road
to the nearby bordello where his favorite whore
opened her present and fainted. He would

have bled to death if Gauguin hadn't hauled him
to hospital next morning. Even in "Self-Portrait
with Bandaged Ear," his necessary color washes in
despite greatcoat and pipe. Science has a word—
xanthopsia—for when objects appear
more yellow than they really are but who's
to say? As yellow as they are, they are.

HOWL REVISITED

. . . in Rockland where we are great writers
on the same dreadful typewriter
I am Kirilov, Carl Solomon said.
I am Prince Myshkin, Ginsberg answered,
serving eight months there instead of jail
for fencing stolen goods for some of his pals,
a plea arranged by two of his professors.

Some say the Kirilov claim was muttered
as Solomon came to from electroshock
and Ginsberg, overhearing, lobbed one back.
Or was it widdershins? Told by another,
it's Dostoevsky in a tennis match

where Allen introduces himself first
as the noble idiot, then depressive Carl
declares that he's the fiery nihilist
who kills himself to prove he has free will
under the tubercular sky surrounded
by orange crates of theology or is this tale
downbeat, beatific, apocryphal?

ON SPEAKING TERMS

Try to come from a large family,
the essayist counsels, so you can stay
on speaking terms with some of them.
I chose the brother
who died of ALS three years after
the first dropped glass shattered
open the last of his life, the one
who begged me to put finis with a pillow
over his head, begged me with words
and when words failed him with gestures
drawing our ancestral carving knife
across his throat with the one hand
that still worked but I knew
his faltering Darwinian engine
could still fling me off and I was a coward.
After him the others fell
in a row, obedient tin soldiers
sun glinting off their helmeted heads
leaving me an ancient orphan
like the ivory bill *very close to extinction*
if not already extinct with its one note
the high false sound of a clarinet
calling, calling unanswered.

MOURNERS, ONLOOKERS, GAWKERS

Thomas Hardy was borne into the Poets' Corner
at Westminister without his heart. Rumor
had it eaten by the surgeon's cat
perched on the mortuary slab as it
awaited burial and a pig's substituted
to be interred in the old churchyard
as the great man had requested: *at Stinsford
I shall sleep quite calmly, whatever happens.*

Some sources said the King of Pop had planned
to have his ashes sprinkled on the moon but
by the time he died his estate could not
finance the trip, and that for pallbearers
he had in mind the Harlem Globetrotters
but his brothers bore the casket at the end.
He lies in the Great Mausoleum at Forest Lawn
with scores of Hollywood's half-remembered stars:
Jean Harlow, Spencer Tracy, Carole Lombard.

The eminent of his day, including J. M. Barrie
Shaw, Kipling, and A. E. Housman, carried
Hardy's cremated remains into the Abbey
past grieving but respectful crowds to lie

next to the grave of Charles Dickens. This
gruesome but historic compromise
was offered by the Stinsford vicar, wise
to Hardy's pride in his working-class family
despite his having called God "that vast imbecility."

Michael Jackson, after years of doctoring
turned from cute African American into a being
of indeterminate gender, whiter than Wasp, one
wisp of hair hanging, nose narrowed, lips reddened
chin cleft, and doubtless more refinements. Retailers
around the world rejoiced in the posthumous fervor.

Tess was bad enough but *Jude* so deeply vexed
the Victorian age's views of God and sex
that the Bishop of Wakefield burned it. Demeaned
and outraged by the epithet *Jude the Obscene*
Hardy responded to the public outcry
by abandoning fiction and taking up poetry.

An audience of millions watched Jackson's funeral
online as the LAPD scrambled to control
the crowds. In Stinsford all shops went

black, blinds drawn for the hour of interment.
So have these two performances a classic likeness?
Do mourners, onlookers, gawkers share a sense
of schadenfreude as the procession passes?
Farewell, Michael, with umbrella and sunglasses.
Vale, Thomas, heartless and staunchly godless.

SEEING THINGS

Why is my brain doing this? I ask the retinologist,
a specialist in the disease that wiped my central
vision away, leaving me with a landscape
through which a tornado has passed, taking my face
when I look in the mirror, taking words on a page,
hands on a clock, taking the great blue who guards
the pond, the spots that freckled the twin fawns
who were still fearless and came nearly as close
to me as you are at your end of this table, I see
a warm blur of your shape before you are crowded out
by visions, sometimes a great huddle of people,
ghostly presences flickering on and offstage, sometimes
crowded patterns multicolored as a wash of banners
at a demonstration, sometimes cobblestone walls overlaid
with brick that haunt my foreground, middle- and background
sometimes mere fleurs-de-lys or enlarged asterisks.

What you have, he tells me, are harmless visual
hallucinations. They are the product of a mentally
healthy brain that is filling in the blanks in your sight.
Nobody knows the how or wherefor. Nobody has a cure.
When I go blind, I ask him, will I still see them?
—They will always be with you, he said. Try to befriend them.

THE WOMEN RETURN FROM DIGGING ROOTS IN THE KALAHARI

Elizabeth Marshall Thomas, *The Old Way*

"Night falls quickly.
Soon the sky in the east has turned deep blue.
In the west the crescent moon is showing
and long red streaks of sunset clouds
lie over the darkening horizon. The air
is cooling noticeably. The first stars appear.
We trudge on not speaking. Even
the children are quiet, perfectly quiet.
Then the new baby whimpers, a tiny sound
and her mother hitches her around to nurse
on the move. In the silent veldt I feel
the night wind rising and hear the whisper
of the grass and the footsteps of the women.
A bat flies over us. A little later we hear
a flock of guinea fowl calling intermittently
as they fly one by one up to their roost
in a tree. Later still a jackal calls
and another answers. The first jackal calls again.
The world of the day is closing. The world
of the night is opening. We keep walking."

lineated with permission of the author

THE LAST WORD

It's a winner
but how
do you get
it in without
jimmying
the lock when
the argument
crescendoes
and reason
lies prone,
winded?

There you are
up against
the door
when suddenly
passion
flings it open
and calmly,
calmly
you walk in.

TRUTH

Came varnished,
prepackaged, required
scissors to break the seal.
Worn raw from use, reuse
it put up splinters.
I sanded it, wiped it
clear with turpentine.
Liked the look of it
newborn. Thought about
polyurethane, two coats
at least—varnish is old hat.
Rethought the climate:
cutting, quick to punish.
Went out for more varnish.

V

AH, POETRY

Whenever I lead a poetry
workshop I tell the would-be poets
to leave all mention of poems

out of their tender tentative poems.
I don't tell them I'm writing a poem
on the forbidden subject of writing poetry

after I've told them to leave the subject of poems
out of their poems. Poems about poetry
are passionless, pointless, passé poems

although looking back through my own old poems
I see I have written *the symbol inside this poem*
is my father's feet . . . Ah, poetry. Poems

about it will only be read by other poets
who comprise most of the people at poetry
readings where the poet reading his poems

aloud will recite his self-esteemed poetry
until the audience sleeps. Who listens to poems
with the attentive suspension that poetry

demands? Sigh. We endure, slaves to poetry.

WILLIAM CARLOS WILLIAMS

After prying the resisting
child's mouth open with a tablespoon
both tonsils covered with membranes

sure signs of the dreaded diphtheria
after pneumonias and kidney
failures after forceps deliveries

it is hard to arrive at *this is just*
to say and *so much depends on*
to accept that they flew from the wedge

of time he wrested for his poetry
late and later at night *one occupation*
he said *complements the other*

confirmed by his son who reported
night was his time to roar
never mind that Williams's brother

returned a book of his poems
as vulgar and immoral
forgive the poet's *he was one*

of those fresh Jewish types
you want to kill on sight
overlook the crude asides

about guineas and gypsies
forgive *when the Scotch go crazy*
they are worse than a Latin

and remember him for
his revulsion against fascism
his admiration for the working-class

women whose babies he brought forth
often after hours of harsh labor
and most of all hold fast

the freshness the unadorned
and potent plain American
speech that he saluted in his poems.

PROVINCETOWN, CAPE COD, 1963

I'm a terrestrial person, the famous poet said,
enfolding each of the skinnydippers
climbing the ladder in a generous towel
from the host's larder. We aspirants
sat in a circle, hair still dripping,
each declaiming our half-finished oeuvres,
our endless revisions that night of passion
as the batwings of talent flittered among us
decreeing who swam fastest, who farthest,
who dived down deepest, who shivered unwrapped.

Midnight, everyone starving, a platter
of eggs over easy, runny on toast.
In that tranche of time, narcissists all,
no one a failure, eyes fixed on the quest,
unthinkable, death by drone or sea level,
enforced migrations, suicide bombings.
Who knew we would live to write the worst?
Poetry had once been love and autumn.

THE DAY MY STUDENT TEACHES ME
THAT LIFE IS NOT ART

When in a workshop in a distant city
a student I have never met before
passes out a poem about the night
a man broke into her bedroom
the black wire hairs on his forearms
as he tied her arms above her head
the familiar smell of the pillow he forced
over her face

      one part of me wants to point
out to the class her creative use
of specific detail and the other part wants
to take her in my arms as a mother sister
best friend press woman flesh to woman
flesh and howl with her just howl.

CABBAGES

It's one thing to kill yourself for unrequited love
but you can't do it for hammertoes, digits
thrumming, cocked up like supersize knuckles.

You can't do it for TMJ, no matter that your mouth
won't open, that you can only chew on one side,
that's not enough to die for or for sciatic pain

shooting down one leg, setting your shin on fire,
no reason to leap from the Belvedere
of The Terrace of Infinity on the Amalfi coast

or go outside naked in New Hampshire at six above
and wait for hypothermia to do you in, how long
would that take? Next thing you know, people

will want to die because they're constipated
or have sinusitis. Montaigne said *I want death to find me
planting my cabbages* but that would be in April.

Nobody wants to commit suicide in April even though
it's the cruelest month etcetera, not even the lovelorn,
from Old English *loren*, past participle

of *leosan* (see "lose"): the change of *s* to *r*
due to Verner's law as Karl Verner declared it
in 1875. Oh, better to go to Google any day

to savor derivations as you weep hot tears
than watch the runway lengthening to a blue scream.

EITHER OR

Death, in the orderly procession
of random events on this gradually
expiring planet crooked in a negligible

arm of a minor galaxy adrift among
millions of others bursting apart in
the amnion of space, *will*, said Socrates,

be either a dreamless slumber without end
or a migration of the soul from one place
to another, like the shadow of smoke rising

from the backroom woodstove that climbs
the trunk of the ash tree outside
my window and now that the sun is up

down come two red squirrels and a nuthatch.
Later we are promised snow.
So much for death today and long ago.

GOING DOWN

They call it *climigration*, these
experts on vast shoreline loss
and islands swept by rising seas.

So far it's minimal. In Papua
New Guinea, a string of seven atolls
are awash. Three thousand souls

are being relocated to a
famous island, Bougainville,
wrested from Japan in World War II.

The tundra that protects the Eskimo
village of Newtok from the Bering Sea
is gradually eroding as the glue

of permafrost beneath it thaws
and arctic water levels rise.
They're going down and so

are all the rest of us—
Florida to Bangladesh
Malaysia to Manhattan

where lamplit Central Park will lurch
with Lady Liberty, her torch
aloft, Chinatown, Hell's Kitchen,

SoHo, Harlem, and the Bronx
into the Atlantic Ocean.
Despite outcries of purest angst

dikes won't save the playing field
so blow a kiss to this drowned world.
The gods have spoken: yield.

JUST DESERTS

It is agreed that life as we know it must come to the end of its tether
by global warming or nuclear winter or whatever

seizure befalls nor will it be humans who watch the sun's demise
as it sucks Earth, Mars, and Venus inside

itself before it collapses from red giant to white dwarf
and we, supreme products of Darwinian selection, will have morphed

into what? going backward, perhaps, to the amoebae we arose
from more than four billion years ago

up from the cave drawings at Lascaux
from the slaughter of bison and passenger pigeons

from Hiroshima and Nagasaki to lie eyes open
in Keats's *unslumbrous night.*

For however long it takes it will serve us right.

PALLAS'S HORSE

When Pallas is killed in battle
in Book Eleven of the Aeneid
the whole sad column escorting
his body is both ceremonial—

scapulars and shields,
chased gold bas-reliefs
adorning the arms
—and hard with grief,

I think of Black Jack, the riderless horse
led prancing at JFK's funeral,
fully tacked with empty
boots reversed in the stirrups.

In Fitzgerald's version
even Pallas's war-horse weeps
big tears rolling down
to wet his cheeks.

THIS ONE

The setting: moonless, pricked apart by stars.
On the grassy napkin in front of the State House
a threesome with tripods and telescopes.

Two guys loping across from the local pub
stop in midstride. *Yeah,* says the younger,
You better be lookin' for a new planet

'cause this one's fucked.

ALLOW ME

Sudden and quiet, surrounded by friends
—John Milton's way—
But who gets to choose this ordered end
Trim and untattered, loved ones at hand?
—Allow me that day.